What Turns Innocent Kids into Ruthless Killers

Born to Win,
Programmed to Fail

Princeton H. Holt

...DEDICATION...

The king said,

"Find out whose son this young man is"

I Samuel 17:56

He is my son's, son

To my first and long-awaited grandson

PRINCETON Gerald HOLT
"YOUR ROYAL HIGHNESS"
Born July 31, 2016

Published by:

Epiphany Publications

New York, New York

Forward

Advancing inspiring guidance and intuition in an everyday style, this book, in Princeton's unique way, provides knowledge, advice and profound perceptiveness to help the reader understand how to prevent future criminal and self-destructive behavior perpetrated by some youthful offenders. Princeton advocates the need to start early in the parenting process to instill values in children by precept and example. He emphasizes what psychologists and behavioral scientists often overlook, and that is the spiritual development of the child. Based on the author's many years of pastoral experience, community organizing, as someone who crafts theater productions and speaks at inner-city schools, the book deals with issues faced by parents and their children in an environment bereft of moral values.

Pastor Holt sets out to stop the pattern before it starts and offers other alternate views of what it truly means to be a productive male, such as educational achievements, community connection and involvement, and a proper sense of one's own dignity and integrity. His passion to provide guidance for parents and encouragement for young people has driven him to write this book.

Emerson G. Miller, Th.D. MSW, LCSW

What Turns Innocent Kids into Ruthless Killers by longtime friend, Princeton H. Holt, is a fresh approach to a chronic problem. How did our families and children get in such poor condition? Holt explores and explains how society has gone from the productive toward the destructive and how its deformation can be transformed for its own betterment. You don't have to go to church or join a religious organization to understand the how-to for applying spiritual values to secular conditions that baffle and seem to be beyond restoration. If you read this book with an open mind, you will learn how you have and all of us have contributed to our desperate condition and also how we can put our families, friends, and relationships back together for the sake of being a blessing and not a burden.

Pastor and Doctor Mark A. McCleary, Founder and President, Mark McCleary Ministries (www.3mmm.org)

Acknowledgements

I want to pause and give a heart-felt thanks to my son Princeton, who walked with me on this journey every step of the way. His advice, resources, and connections were unlimited during this whole process. In my moments of uncertainty as to whether I should press forward or give up on this project, Princeton would not allow my knees to buckle. His faith and confidence in the manuscript and in his dad was the fuel that kept me going. My debt to him is eternal. Then there is Craig Morgan, one who has his ear to the ground and gave me his honest youthful advice in areas where I was out of touch. With much love, I thank you.

Table of Contents

Introduction 1

Chapter 1-.- Born To Win, Programmed To Fail.....................19

Chapter 2-.- The Struggle Between Two Worlds.....................19

Chapter 3-.- Atmosphere – Climate - Culture 36

Chapter 4-.- Where It Started Going Downhill 44

Chapter 5-.- America Has A Culture Problem: Hip Hop 52

Chapter 6-.- The Music Has Gone Too Far........................61

Chapter 7-.- Believing And Living A Lie 68

Chapter 8-.- The Profile Of A Teenage Killer.....................75

Chapter 9-.- The Only Place Where Truth Is Found 84

Chapter 10-.- The Problem Can Be Fixed 96

-About The Author-...99

Introduction

(A Must Read)

To be born or not to be born, you had no choice. Who your mom and dad would be, you had no choice, the atmosphere and culture, in your home, responsible for the programming and conditioning of your delicate and undeveloped mind, you had no choice. The neighborhood and the kids you grew up with, were not yours to choose.

Looking back over your life, at the multiple failures, the countless disappointments, the unforeseen setbacks, and the insurmountable roadblocks, if you had a choice, knowing what you now know, you might have chosen different parents. If you had a choice, knowing what you now know, you might have chosen a different home culture and a more upscale neighborhood and friends. If you had a choice, knowing what you now know, and where your mistakes have landed you in life, some of you might have chosen not to have been born at all.

This book is a revelation of how innocent babies from all walks of life, and every ethnic background, who did not choose to come here, enter this deranged, broken world, wired to win but are programmed to fail. There is an adverse, rebel, gangster culture in American that swallows up innocent kids, without their conscious consent or awareness.

Even good kids from good homes are being misinformed and misguided by misinformation. This misinformation does not begin in their preschool or kindergarten classroom. It does not come when the child is introduced to the language of their parents. It is not introduced in the form of spoken words or fictitious teaching.

The misinformation becomes ingrained in the child, inside the home in the form of a toxic atmospheric condition, created by ill-informed parents, way before the baby is born.

You will see that the hidden message in this book is not altogether about innocent children who become ruthless killers. It is also about you, with references made comparing you and the similarities in the life of Kashawn Davis, who is on death row for taking the lives of two neighborhood acquaintances.

You will be given deep insights into your own life's journey, and the ramifications of your upbringing. This book will provide a glimpse into the seen world and the unseen world, the inner you and the outer you.

The same tools used in Kashawn's development during his formative years, were the same tools used in yours. Dysfunction, in one form or another, is part of all families because all are born into a broken world, filled with broken people and raised by broken parents. From this, there is no escape.

No child comes into the world cursing, being disrespectful, or violent. These are all learned behaviors. My goal is to share with parents, educators, and child service providers, how this adverse culture is programming innocent children during their formative years and the impact that the home plays in this process. I will also inject, on a side note, how the hip-hop culture has impacted all of society, directly or indirectly, and how this culture has assisted in turning innocent babies into deviant rebels of society.

In no way do I intend to minimize the effect that video games, movies, poverty, racism, birth abnormalities, and many other factors have on our children's healthy development. Neither do I desire to villainize the masterful art form of rap music in its purest rendering. So please don't overlook this insertion. Anyone with eyes can readily see the genius and the creative skills behind this genre of music.

My only intention is to highlight its destructive elements and what it's doing to our children before they even have a choice in the direction of their lives.

Even though there is no excuse for the lives that were taken and the families dismantled because of Kashawn's reckless choices, I am going to run the risk of speaking in his defense, especially during those formative years when his programming and conditioning became embedded. I take this position because I have some inside information that I want to share, simply because I believe there is another part of Kashawn's story that is not being told.

I want to make it very clear that this is not an academic rendering about the above stated problem. Neither is this coming from the pen of a scholar on the subject. I am a Man of God, an Ordained Minister of the Gospel, with no less authority. One who has spiritual insight into an epidemic that I believe deserves some spiritual applications. This is an opinion presentation and it should be taken as such.

DON'T BLAME THE CHILDREN

We read in the papers and hear on the air

Of killing and stealing and crime everywhere

We sigh and we say as we notice the trend

This young generation oh where will it end

But can we be sure that it's their fault alone

That maybe apart of it isn't our own

Are we less guilty who place in their way?

Too many things that lead them astray?

Too much money to spend, too much idle time

Too many movies of passion and crime

Too many books not fit to be read

A diet of evil they're constantly fed

Too many children encouraged to roam

By too many parents who won't stay at home

Now kids don't make the movies

And they don't write the books

That paint bad pictures of gangsters and crooks

They don't make the drugs that mess up the brain

It's all done by older folks greedy for gain

Delinquent teenagers oh how we condemn

The sins of the nation and blame it on them

But by the law of the blameless the Savior made known

Who is there amongst us to cast the first stone?

In so many cases it sad but it's true

That the title delinquent fits older folks too.

Sammy Davis Jr. (1928-1990)

What Turns Innocent Kids Into Ruthless Killers?

Chapter One

Born to Win, Programmed to Fail

1

Born to Win, Programmed to Fail

Before the Beginning Began

I want to take you on an imaginary journey that takes us back in time way before the beginning of the world began. A time when there was no solar system, no planets, no earth, no continents, no nations, no cities, no people, no houses, no animals, no plants, no NOTHING.

Everything that now is, only existed in the mind of God as a figment of His imagination. God had an idea. All things that we see and enjoy in this world started as an idea. This idea spinning around in God's head, developed into a dream and from that dream into a vision. God's dream was to create human beings in his likeness and for them to be housed in a perfect environment void of evil and corruption.

This perfect place would accommodate their every need and purpose. It would fuel their quest for adventure, while fulfilling an innate compulsion to create and develop an undeveloped world that would bring glory to God. This place of habitation would be called Earth, a place with all the essential resources, seen and unseen, that would be necessary to fulfill God's vision for humankind.

Selected Before the Foundation of the World

Like a soon to be bride, wearing a nightgown, sitting at her nightstand compiling a list of guests to invite to her wedding ceremony, God sits in conference with members of the Godhead to compile a list of unborn and unnamed people He would choose to favor with the gift we all call LIFE. Many were chosen to be on that list: people of the past, present, and future, but many were not. What went into the selection process? We do not know.

As we peek over God's shoulder, we strain anxiously to see if we are included on that list. In the process of our search we are immediately drawn to the discovery that Kashawn Davis, an innocent child turned killer, was on that list. He was in good company, because Oprah Winfrey, Bill Gates, Barack Obama, John F. Kennedy, you, and, thank God, me, along with a slew of others, were also added to that list by a loving God.

Kashawn was on God's mind before the foundation of the world and was awarded God's greatest gift to man - LIFE. A gift that billions of the unthought-of, and the unborn, will never get a chance to experience or enjoy. Kashawn Davis was God's crowning act of creation. God is always at his best when performing a creative act, especially when that act involves human life.

Born to Win

All kids, whether black or white, rich or poor, gang member or Harvard University graduate, enter the world the same way; pure, innocent, and undefiled, with a blank brain hard drive and no data entry. All children, Kashawn Davis included, came into this foreign and contaminated world searching for identity, needing to belong, wanting to be loved, yearning to understand and needing to be understood.

Kashawn was born to win with a complete digestive, nervous, reproductive, circulatory, and skeletal system all perfectly in place and functioning according to design. Even though the odds were against his arrival, because of the millions of sperm that fought for the same singular egg, all of them died off in the process, leaving behind that one sperm that had Kashawn's DNA written all over it. He had defied the odds and that was not by happenstance, but by design.

Blindsided by an Adverse Culture

Like Kashawn Davis, kids who kill don't start life as killers. They are usually judged by how their life ends and not how it begins. Almost all children come into the world wired to win, with a few exceptions due to birth abnormalities, but overall, most all kids are wired to win. The sheer fact that they showed up is a winning indication. All the cells in their body are in perfect alignment with all the laws of the universe. Like a flower whose petals reach out like open arms to the sun, every fiber in their body responds to the positive energy of the universe and was never intended to be out of alignment, disfigured or distorted by unseen negative forces around them.

The people around these children were placed in their lives to assist them in their quest and drive to win. But most of these innocent children were blindsided by an adverse, contaminated culture, in the home, which they did not sign up for. Born into a toxic family culture, it placed them in the losing lane before their race even began. They are reaping a harvest that they themselves did not sow. They are caught in a web that they did not spin.

Programmed to Fail

In Central New Jersey, I performed an observation, where I compared ten African-American youth from a high crime area, to fourteen white youth from a wealthy upper-class area. I had always wondered why these two races and classes of youth could like the same type of hip-hop music, but both be affected differently by it. Without their knowledge of what I was doing, I accompanied both groups at different times, to and from a hip-hop concert in southern New Jersey.

The African-American group was rowdy and profane to and from the concert. They were mirroring the behavior of the rappers they had just gone to see in word and conduct. On the other hand, the white youth were exposed to the same music, enjoyed it as much as their counterparts, but left the concert with a totally different disposition that was void of the rowdy and profane presented by the first group.

When I shared this outcome with my daughter, she wanted to know what made the difference. I told her the difference was the soil into which both groups were planted. If the soil or culture in the home is toxic, then the child's behavior will be toxic. However, if the soil in the home is well attended, then the behavior will reflect the texture of the soil. Let me hasten to say that no family is exempt from dysfunction, rich or poor, but some families are more dysfunctional than others and in most cases with different outcomes.

Toxic Soil Defined

Toxic soil, in this instance, can be defined as a culture in the home, contaminated by parents who are unaware of how their negative behavior affects the atmospheric condition in the household. These parents are not very nice to each other, their behavior and attitude is so appalling it makes the children around them suffer and become appalling as well.

Contamination in the home does not have to be blatant, it could be very subtle but damaging, nevertheless. Most parents are oblivious to what their home culture is or that there even is one. In many families, there is no recognizable code of conduct, nor any distinct values or belief system that they are aware of. It is something they never think about nor does it come up in any conversation. They live life by the seat of their pants. If you don't have moral values to govern your child's conduct, then the popular rebel culture outside of the home will define your child's behavior for you, and you may not be satisfied with the outcome.

Products of Our Environment

Every person who has influenced our life has a point of view and shares with us what he sees the way he sees it. A parent's point of view may not always be verbally spoken but is always demonstrated by how that parent behaves and lives.

Just by living your life from day to day, functional or dysfunctional, you are living it from your point of view. This is non-verbal communication. It shows up in your attitude and your disposition towards people, places and things, without you speaking a word. You don't have to say you dislike someone. It shows up in your attitude towards them. You don't have to say you are afraid of dogs or insects. It shows up in your attitude towards them.

Your kids are watching, and what they see in your disposition toward people and the world around you overrides what you say. They are programmed through your non-verbal communication, as well as verbal, and they mimic what they see in you. Your disposition around your spouse, your attitude towards police officers and your child's teacher, shows up without words. You are the model they will grow to become.

This is what I meant when I said children are misinformed and misguided by misinformation. This misinformation and programming come in more than just one way. What you dislike, your fears, what disturbs you impacts the child. He will mirror the things he sees in you. Keep in mind, the way you understand and relate to God, yourself, others, and the world in which you live, will establish your worldview.

Your point of view is the culmination of all these factors mixed together. If you don't have a healthy concept of God, yourself, and others, your life will always have missteps and major challenges. Wrong decisions could be made, which will inevitably lead to an undesirable end.

Let me repeat what I stated earlier: every person who has influenced our life has a point of view and shares with us what he sees the way he sees it. Knowledge is always given to us from the giver's point of view, whether that knowledge is credible or not, founded upon truth or error. No child comes into the world cursing, being disrespectful, or violent. These are all learned behaviors.

During our formative years (ages 0-7) we take on the thought patterns and belief system of those around us who we respect. We inherit what they believe, right or wrong, and it becomes the foundation of our worldview. If a child's parents are Muslim or Christian, the child inherits that worldview without having a choice in the matter. If a child's parents are white supremist or Satanist, then the child grows up believing the same.

If when you're born, your mother tells you that the blue sky above you is red, then to you, the blue sky is red. The more the red sky is discussed in your family circle, the more embedded this erroneous information becomes until it forms a stronghold in your brain, and you become bound by those thought patterns. Even though the information is false, it becomes your system of belief, your worldview; the misinformation comes from a source that you believe to be reliable, but is actually unreliable. The person who shares this faulty information probably believes that the information he shares is true, but he too has been deceived.

The negative culture outside of the home, the profane music, and violent friends, only adds to his deviate behavior. When he becomes old enough to make choices on his own, it is too late, the damage has been done. He would have to encounter a paradigm shift that changes how he thinks and in what he believes for change to take place in his life. In my world it is called a conversion.

That's why I can comfortably stand on the right side of Kashawn Davis and speak in his defense. During his formative years, he was not able to make choices on his own and I therefore declare his innocence. The atmospheric condition and culture in the home, in most cases, laid the foundation for whom he would become. Much of what children reap by the time they start kindergarten, they never planted, somebody else did. The sacred responsibility of parenting is often not realized by many parents and they often raise their children by default.

The damaged child who needs the most love will demand it in the most unloving way. If others have sown tares in the child's field, there is no way around reaping a negative outcome. The child is caught in a web that he did not spin.

Those so-called good kids who come from good homes, who go astray, are exposed to negative programming in the form of unkind words, unhealthy conversations, negative dispositions, attitudes, and behaviors in the home that creates a pattern of thinking in the child's head that may not be easily broken.

Parents as Gatekeepers

Kashawn Davis was born perfectly complete in one way but drastically incomplete in another. He was complete with body parts and internal systems functioning according to design but was incomplete when it came to brain development. This part of him needed to be developed to a high level of functionality to enable him to be a productive blessing to God, himself, and humanity.

Your home provides the work place, the manufacturing plant, where the child is brought from dependence to independence. Then the child who is now an adult, is presented to the world where only independence is respected.

Parents are the gatekeepers to their children's souls, especially during those early years. During ancient times gatekeepers would stand guard at the gate of the palace, watching and protecting against any enemies who might approach the city and endanger the life of the King and his subjects.

When an enemy would approach the city, the gatekeepers would close the gates to prevent entrance to anyone who would attempt to do harm to the Kingdom. However, they would allow entrance to anyone who would do the Kingdom well. So, as gatekeepers, parents must guard the windows of their children's souls, protecting them from any influence that might contaminate and ruin their delicate spirit and their futures.

Chapter Two

The Struggle Between Two Worlds

2
The Struggle Between Two Worlds

The Seen and the Unseen

Kashawn Davis is a product of two worlds: the seen world and the unseen world, also known as the physical and the spiritual worlds. The unseen world is more real than the seen world, because the unseen world brought the seen world into visibility.

Kashawn is made up of an inner man and an outer man. The inner man, though unseen, is who he really is. The outer man, the physical man, is just the house that the inner man lives in.

The breakdown in all relationships can be found when the inner child is overlooked in the programming process and by default forms into a personality that is at odds with the world around him. We must give close attention to the inner or spiritual development of the child. It supersedes the outer development for it focuses on his relationships to people and the world he lives in. Healthy relationships must be formed with God, self, and others in order for happiness to be achieved. Many people miss this important consideration and area of development.

Lastly, there is head knowledge and spiritual knowledge. Head knowledge can be acquired through reading, writing, and arithmetic. Spiritual insight or knowledge, on the other hand, is acquired from the spirit world and is activated from the atmosphere, climate, and culture in which you are planted. It is the atmosphere and culture that programs the inner man and it can be either positive or negative. The inner world and outer world must all work together to produce a fully developed child.

There are rich and educated people who have it all together on the outside, but have many forms of dysfunction on the inside. Their relationships in their home, and with others, have much to be desired. They have eyes but can't see, ears but can't hear, and minds but don't understand.

God created all of us, three-dimensional. We are body, soul, and spirit. Society is quick to acknowledge the presence and operations of the body (health and wellness) and soul (intellect, emotions, and will) but give little or no credence to the spirit of man. As you will see, all three dimensions must be treated equally during those formative years, or else we will grow adults who are only 2/3 complete with the other 1/3, in a state of disarray. I believe that the 1/3 of us that is left unattended is the spiritual or relational part of us.

You can be highly educated with many degrees behind your name. You may have years of experience in a specific field of discipline, but when 1/3 of your development has been overlooked, it destroys your ability to experience healthy relationships with God and others. The education of the head does not develop the inner man. Neither does it teach you how to have healthy relationships. The child who misbehaves is fractured in his relationship with his parents and the world around him and it happens during his formative years.

Both the inner you and the outer you were designed by God to participate in the development of your world. Just like the physical part of you has eyes to see and ears to hear, so does the inner you. Your inner man, or spirit, sees and hears what your physical ears and eyes can't. When you walk into a room filled with opposition or danger, you can't see the opposition or danger, no one tells you that it's there, but you can feel it. In this case, your spirit-man is activated.

You can't see love, kindness, or respect with your physical eyes, but these things are tangible elements in the unseen world and can be perceived and produced by the inner man and placed on display, through the physical man, for the outer world to see and experience.

Your head doesn't teach you how to love. Love comes from the inner man or from the heart. God is love and God is a Spirit. Therefore, the spirit of man, when connected with God's Spirit, becomes a reflection of who and what God is and what He intends us to be. The outer man doesn't teach you how to share, be kind, or respectful. It doesn't teach you the need of maintaining a healthy relationship with the God who created you. It doesn't teach you how to be secure in your own skin or to feel like you belong. This is the spiritual part of your conditioning, and it takes place in your heart and not your head.

When we closely examine the behavior of many politicians on Capitol Hill, with their degrees in law, political science, economics, and finance, you would think that with their combined knowledge and experiences, they would be able to fix the problems of the world.

The sad fact is that their experience and intellect is not the problem that prohibits them from solving national and international issues. Head knowledge and experience is necessary, and that they have, but it's the development of the heart that is lacking. Deprived during childhood of that relationship building period, it is this neglect that has severely handicapped most of these politicians and now while serving on Capital Hill, shows up in how the govern.

If you look beneath the surface, you will see that the problem in Washington is about politicians who seem not to know how to build healthy relationships with one another. Relational issues, not attended to in childhood, develops adults who do not know how to trust, love, respect or care.

They are always in conflict with one another. Conflict is a sign of brokenness.

Divisiveness, greed, and racism could be the outcome of one who has not developed properly in his relational growth and has missed some steps after coming out of his mother's womb. The child with the frown on his face or the kid who won't let others play with his toys has been flawed during the developmental process. I see the same childish activities playing out in Washington by politicians who act like sixty- or seventy-year-old babies who refuse to grow up.

Love Grows Up

The Apostle Paul said in I Cor.13:11 *"When I was a child, I spoke as a child, I understood as a child, I thought as a child: but when I became a man, I put away childish things."*

Children become very upset over any personal harm. For example, if a pin pricks the skin, the child will cry as if they have been deadly wounded. They are not concerned about the suffering of others; they weep mostly for themselves. Children want to be the center of attention. They are willing to play if they can choose the game. They demand applause and appreciation.

Children owe nobody anything. Their attitude is to get all they can, but they have little obligation to any other person. Children rarely think of what they owe their parents or society. Children are completely self-centered. They live in a world that revolves around them. Many of our politicians, not all, have a lot of growing up to do.

There is no problem that love and respect can't fix. If the two political parties in Washington would be genuinely concerned about the welfare of each other and the people they serve, they could find a way to fix a broken government or at least make it better. Just like a trained mechanic can fix a broken car, or the engineers at NASA can send a man to the moon, head knowledge and heart knowledge working together will find a way to fix a broken world.

The only reason why the world is broken is because of broken people. People are broken because of a fracture in one or more of their relationships. Mend relationships fix the broken world. It's all about the inner development of humankind.

A Spiritual Approach to Things

Don't be alarmed or skeptical by these spiritual assertions. I know they are not popular. When a person alludes to spiritual inclusion in helping to solve earthly problems, his argument is immediately dismissed as unintelligible. People find it hard to believe what can't be seen.

But to exclude the unseen spiritual function is to miss the major reason for Kashawn's dysfunction. It puts his future at risk, especially when many other solutions to his problems have not been working to our satisfaction. Spiritual things are just as real as material things and there are spiritual realities as well as material realities. There is a spirit man inside of you, a truth I'm sure you will not deny. It is the missing link that leads the innocent child down the road to self-destruction because he is out-of-sync with his relational-self.

The child's relationship with his parents in childhood had been fractured before he could even speak, and his parents were not even aware of it. It is the cause of the child's relational breakdown with everything around him. He does not know how to relate to himself, his parents, his teachers, to rules and regulations or society in general. His problem is relational.

The intangible spiritual elements that God has provided must be a deliberate part of conditioning during the formative years. One focuses on the head and the other focuses on the heart. That's why both the physical you and the spiritual you must grow and work together, as you will need both to be a healthy and complete 3/3's of a human being.

When I first mentioned the body, soul, and spirit, you may have noticed that I said little or nothing about the soul of man. Not that the soul doesn't play a major part, but my spiritual focus needs to take center stage. When the spirit is in place, the soul will automatically follow suit.

The Reality of the Unseen

I cannot introduce the inner and outer you, the physical and spiritual world, without introducing the spiritual God. He is the Creator and center of all things. Human beings were created in God's image after His likeness. We love because God loves. We are perceptive because God perceives. We are creative because God creates. We were created in the image of God after His likeness.

He is also the Creator of the seen and unseen worlds, but He operates in the seen world, from an unseen position. Sometimes God seems so very far away. That is by design. God hides Himself only to be discovered. He said in the book of Jeremiah 29:13: *"You will seek me and find me when you search for me with all your heart."*

I believe God creates unseen things and hides them in the universe just for us to discover them. Hidden truth once revealed is transformative in nature. It causes an epiphany, a paradigm shift, an a-ha moment, a moment of sudden insight or discovery. This happens when a person experiences a spiritual conversion, when old things are passed away and all things become new. This experience God desires for us all. Life is filled with many of these a-ha moments. It's God's way of growing us from the inside out. Seeing something one way but suddenly seeing it from a totally different perspective has the power to change how a person sees the world. It is a renewing of the mind, which is transformative within itself.

Look at matter, atoms, electrons, and neutrons, for instance. These are unseen building blocks in the universe, hidden things placed there by God to be discovered and used by brilliant scientists who are created in the image of God, with the knowledge to bring things that are not seen into visibility. For them, these discoveries are a-ha moments.

Everything that you see in the physical world originated in the unseen world in the form of an unseen idea. These ideas were dropped into the Earth's realm from a Divine Source and lands into the minds of many earthlings.

Many people who receive the idea are not prepared to develop it because the soil of their mind is cluttered with thorns and thistles and the cares of this life, so the idea cannot take root, and it dies. The idea only hatches in the minds of those who possess good fertile soil prepared with knowledge, resources, and discipline that can bring an unseen idea into fruition.

It is God who set these two worlds into motion. It is His intent that we discover the relational building blocks in the unseen world and use what we find to build a physical and spiritual oneness with Him, with people, places and things.

Oneness brings us all together as one big global family working in harmony for the good of the whole.

Because He is Spirit, God is invisible to the natural eye. But because you cannot see a thing does not mean that thing does not exist. Your inability to see your inner man does not mean that your inner man does not exist.

Right now, in the room where you sit, there are music waves in the air that cannot be heard with the natural ear. There are also color images in the air that you cannot see with the natural eye. The reason you can't see them is because you don't have the proper apparatus necessary to plug into that frequency.

Scientists have discovered a way to harness those unheard music waves along with those unseen color images and transmit them through wires in your walls so that they appear on your television screen and stereo system in your living room. Just because you cannot see a thing does not mean it doesn't exist. God is at work in our lives and He develops us and programs us through healthy atmospheric conditions.

There is also an outlaw spirit in our world, whose mission is to misinform, mislead, and misguide parents and their children leading them to a destructive destination. This distortion of information creates a contaminated culture that leads innocent children in the opposite direction of what God intended. This adverse spirit also aims to distort, pervert, and destroy everything that God had made good.

This foul spirit stands in the delivery room, waiting for the mother to deliver an innocent child, so he can devour it as soon as he is born. Before the child can tell the difference between right and wrong, and before he can choose which way to go, he is immersed in a contaminated, adverse culture that swallows him up and he is not aware that he is being swallowed up. He can't define what's happening around him. He can't speak, he does not understand. His spirit knows that something is not right, but the child can't say "NO" to the negative influences that his spirit repels.

He is bound by the circumstances that he finds himself in, so he succumbs. "Gotcha," says that foul spirit, rendering the child defenseless. By the time he can make choices for himself, it's too late; someone has already made those choices for him. He now defines the world through his parent's point of view, and sees things the way he has been programmed to see them.

Hosea 4:6: *"My people are being destroyed for lack of knowledge."* And it breaks God's heart.

We all need to be aware of these spiritual and unseen forces and use the knowledge to our advantage as we navigate through life, raising families, and living in peace with one another. Without this insight, we could very well end up as damaged goods. Especially if we want to make sense out of how we behave.

Chapter Three

Atmosphere
Climate - Culture

3
Atmosphere
Climate - Culture

Culture is not something you can actually see. It is the behavior of a family or group that has been shaped by their belief system and values. It's what causes members of a family to co-exist. It governs the way they treat each other. If the parents have a worldview that is distorted by the family they grew up in, they will usually bring their malfunction into the lives of their children.

The culture around you can either be your friend or your enemy. It can make you or destroy you. Open your spiritual eyes when you join a group, a club, a church, or begin a new job. Become aware of the atmosphere and climate around you. Determine if it's a healthy or unhealthy place. If it's unhealthy or toxic, you can run from it or live to change it.

To stay in it, you could become adversely affected by it, because of the weakness of your inner man. To hang in there, you can also decide to purposefully change the atmosphere, which could very well be your contribution to a broken world. A smile on your face, an encouraging word, a compliment here and there, a positive attitude will go a long way to impact the negative space that you occupy.

"You are the salt of the earth; you are the light of the world. Let your light so shine that men may see your good works and glorify your God which is in heaven."

Matt 5:13-16

Unseen tools produce atmospheres and cultures. These unseen tools were provided by an unseen God for the purpose of creating atmospheric conditions that lead to a healthy and productive lifestyle. Only you can create the climate and culture in your home that will determine the success and happiness of your family.

The Tools of Engagement

God honored his part of the plan by favoring Kashawn with the gift of life, but he entrusted the next stage of Kashawn's development to the hands of his parents. The culture in the home is the furnace where the programming and conditioning of a child's mind and heart takes place. Tools that are at your disposal to create culture are in the world of unseen things. These tools are thoughts, thought patterns, words, values, and beliefs.

Your first tool is your thought patterns. When your thought patterns are sustained, or when they become a pattern of the way you think, it forms into your disposition or attitude. If your thought patterns are negative your disposition will be negative. Your body language, your facial expressions will reflect your thought patterns. That negative disposition affects the atmospheric conditions in the home, which over a period affects the spirit and disposition of your child.

So-called well-to-do families, who don't share the same toxic culture that poverty bears on the inner-city family, will not escape the damage done to their children by their conflicting attitudes towards each other. Their children will also be damaged.

The funky disposition in a negative parent breeds a funky disposition in your child. Now your funky child goes to school with a funky attitude. You gave him this malignant disease that he doesn't know how to fix, and neither do you, putting his teacher and students at risk. If this is your problem, my new book coming soon, will help get you out of this situation and will equip you with what is needed to turn your child's behavior around.

The second tool to keep in mind is the proper use of words. Words have creative power. They can either bless or curse. They can build up a person or tear them down. Water is a gift from God and when it is properly used, it will grow the trees that give oxygen for the air that we breathe, it gives moisture to the ground which provides the food that we eat. But out of control, that same water that gives life can flood our homes, drown our babies, and can even destroy our lives.

The greater a thing's potential for good when used rightly, the greater its potential for evil when used wrongly. No word is without power. Something happens in the universe with every word that you speak. Words of love, kindness, encouragement, affirmation, faith, and respect not only programs the spirit of the child, but also creates the atmosphere and culture in the home in which the child is being raised.

The third tool is your core values that governs the behavior patterns of the people in your home. They create boundaries. Core values will tell you how to act with your friends, and in all other relationships. A child who determines not to have sex before marriage and holds to it, has chosen that as a core value.

The fourth tool is to establish a belief system in your home that is ethical and moral in nature. When all these elements are rightly understood and put to work, your child will be reared in a wholesome culture, which will give him a fighting chance to resist the negative influences in the world when there are no parents around.

Changing the Culture

Cultures can be changed or created. It only takes a few people who think alike, believe alike, and behave alike, over an extended period of time, to create or change a culture. It can be done deliberately, or it is done by default without people knowing that it is being done.

All cultures begin atmospherically. An atmosphere that is sustained over time becomes a climate. Climates that are sustained become culture and cultures produce strongholds. Let me elaborate by explaining how the atmosphere works in our lives.

I was up speaking to an audience one evening, and there was a person in the audience who was in strong opposition to my point of view. He didn't have to tell me he was in opposition, I could pick up on his thought patterns in the atmosphere. I could feel his conflicting spirit by his facial expression and body language, and I avoided eye contact with him for the rest of my speech because to look at him would have allowed his thought patterns to interfere with my inner man.

If a lot of people in the audience shared an oppositing point of view, then the conflicting thought patterns of the many would have created a stronghold in the atmosphere. It would have been difficult for me to continue.

Have you ever walked into a room and soon as you entered the people stopped talking to each other and immediately you could sense that they had been talking about you? This happens because thought patterns are still lingering in the air. Thought patterns are spiritual and can create a positive or negative atmosphere. It shows up in the disposition of a person. Your thought patterns form dispositions and others can pick it up. Your disposition is your unseen spirit on display through your personage.

The Apostle Paul says in Eph. 2:2 that *"Satan is the prince of the power of the air"* or the prince of atmospheric conditions.

An atmosphere is both physical (weather related) and spiritual, and both are unseen. In this chapter, I will deal with the spiritual implications of the atmosphere and its impact on the child's life.

Paul's words indicate that Satan dominates the atmosphere, both physical and spiritual. Satan starts his domination and mission of destruction in our lives by poisoning and contaminating the atmosphere that's around us. He begins this vicious attack on us at birth. It is from this spiritual unseen position of power that he controls the behavior of people, families, neighborhoods, cities, and nations. The atmosphere where you dwell will eventually become the culture of your dwelling place. Your culture formulates your frame of reference, your likes and dislikes, the decisions you make and why, how you see the world and how you behave.

Spiritual atmospheres can be felt but not seen. When I walk through certain parts of Brownsville, a high crime area in Brooklyn, NY, I feel a sense of danger and uneasiness that I don't feel when I'm walking through Brooklyn Heights, a wealthy section of Brooklyn. The danger felt in Brownsville is caused by violent atmospheric conditioning. The inner man and not the outer man pick up on this condition.

When acts of violence are committed in a neighborhood over and over again, that violent behavior forms a sense of danger in the atmosphere. It becomes embedded and forms a stronghold. Remember, Satan is the prince of the power of the air. It is his sphere of domination.

Satan controls our behavior through the culture that is established around us. In most cases, the culture around us has been poluted by broken people who don't have a clue of how life should be lived. A culture can either build up the people in it or can tear them down. It can give life or breed death.

As a child growing up, when I heard the word stronghold, I was taught to believe it meant satanic bondage. I have since concluded that strongholds are thought patterns. Your thought patterns are what binds, programs, and conditions you, resulting in embedded behavior on autopilot.

Chapter Four

Where It Started Going Downhill

4
Where It Started Going Downhill

Where It All Starts

Have you seen children who, when they start preschool or kindergarten, come to school every day with a frown on their faces, or are in a funky mood for no apparent reason? A child cannot put into context why he feels the way he feels and acts the way that he does. But his spirit knows that something in his outside world is out of alignment with his pure, undefiled spirit.

Something in his home environment is out of harmony with the laws of the universe. When the climate at home is disjointed, it distorts the child's spirit, and that distortion is what you see played out on the child's face and behavior when he comes to school.

The child is bitter, and that bitterness starts developing in the infant way before pre-school or kindergarten begins. It stems from disappointments that the child experiences, not in his head, but in his spirit that accumulates over time. The child's spiritual needs begin in the womb and continue after birth.

There are things that the child's spirit craves for from the spirit of his parents at different intervals during those formative years. In most cases the parents are not even aware of it. Consequently, it leaves the child's spiritual needs unmet. When the spirit of the child is disappointed, and it happens over an extended period time, those disappointments turn into bitterness.

If the child does not feel loved or secure inwardly, then he feels ignored, insecure, like he does not belong. The spirit feels misunderstood and there begins a fracture in the child's perfect world, and a disconnect in his relationship with his parents.

The bitter disappointments in his early days show up in his dysfunction in school and carries over into his adult life. When parents or teachers try to correct his behavior, it is almost impossible, because the behavior is embedded. It is now a stronghold.

Conditioning for Healthy Relationships

Before a child is born, there are things that go on in the home in which notice must be taken; the profane music that's continuiosly played, the television programs sensationalizing violence has an enormous impact on the atmosphere. These modes of activity create a culture in the home that can either be good or bad for your child's development. Are the conversations negative, combative, unkind, critical, profane, demeaning, or are they just the opposite? Whatever they are, they will show up in the atmosphere and will form a culture that will mold your child's behavior.

There are parents who are bitter about having a baby they did not want, at a time they did not want it, and with a person they did not love, or will never see again. Your dissatisfaction unconsciously programs your child, not with words, but through your disposition and attitude. Your child cannot be fooled. His spirit picks up on the negativity that's going on in your personal world and he can be distorted by it.

If your child's conception took place as a result of rape or a one-night stand, you need to know that your baby was not a mistake. Ask Oprah Winfrey, Steve Jobs, Eddie Murphy, Chuck Norris, Barack Obama, Colin Power, Shaquille O'Neal, and Jesse Jackson. All were born out of wedlock and look where they are today. Nothing happens by happenstance. God will take your mistakes and misfortunes and turn them into miracles.

Your child is a child of destiny, born for a reason, to fill a need or to solve a problem, either in the life of one person or in the lives of many. The mere fact that he showed up is a divine indication. Don't breed negativity in your home through your attitude or your disposition because of a child you did not want, or a marriage in conflict or other circumstances that seem undesirable.

The first responsibility of new parents is to focus on a healthy culture in the home so that later in life your child will only partake in healthy relationships. The academic programming of the mind will come full force later on, but now the focus must be on his relational development, something that only parents can adequately provide.

Healthy spiritual programming is the child's first line of defense against a bitter world he soon will be forced to face. If he's prepared, in most cases, he will win, if he's not, in most cases, he will lose. Ensure that the home environment is surrounded by what is necessary to produce positive outcomes.

Without Words

How to communicate to a child without words is a challenge all new parents face. A child does not understand words. He cannot interpret what he sees. All he can decipher is what he feels coming from the spirit of his parents, and what his spiritual senses pick up in his surrounding environment. The home is the first and most important lesson he will receive from the new world he has inherited. He is interpreting the world through the spirit of those around him. Their feelings about things become his feelings about things. His relationship with his parents is a prelude to all of the relationships he will ever have.

The child hears with his spirit, sees with his spirit, thinks with his spirit, and interprets the unseen and seen world with his spirit. You are the first relationship that he will have, it's a spiritual relationship and it must be a healthy one.

When you hold your child, does the child feel your uncertainty about life, your depression, your anxiety, or the grudge you are harboring? What you hold inside shows up in your body language and can be discerned by the spirit of a child.

If the child feels loved, secure, and safe, it can stabilize that child, who will give back to the world what he has received. If the child is not made to feel secure, he becomes insecure. If the child doesn't feel safe or have a sense of belonging, he develops a sense of abandonment, and it is reflected in adulthood. Many people are needy and cling on to others as a result of this deficiency.

Modeling

In a recent poll of adult Americans conducted by the Wall Street Journal, moral decline was slated to be the biggest problem in America. When I was growing up in Brooklyn, NY, our generation had a saying that still rings true today. "Monkey see monkey do." Children pay more attention to what a parent does more than what a parent says. Parents who preach but do not model, have little impact on the behavioral development of the child.

What Turns Innocent Kids Into Ruthless Killers?

Parents must never forget that children learn moral values mainly within their homes and by relying on their parents as role models. When families are unstable or immoral and profane, the learning of moral values within the home is greatly hindered.

According to psychologist Nancy Eisenburg, parents who preach but do not model may have little positive effect on their children's pro-social development. It was Edgar A. Guest who wrote:

> *I would rather see a sermon*
>
> *Than to hear one any day*
>
> *I'd rather one would walk with me*
>
> *Than merely tell the way.*
>
> *The eye's a better pupil*
>
> *And more willing than the ear*
>
> *Fine counsel is confusing*
>
> *But examples always clear*
>
> *And the best of all preachers*
>
> *Are the men who live their creeds?*
>
> *For to see good put in action*
>
> *Is what everybody needs?*
>
> *I best can learn to do it*

If you'll let me see it done

I can watch your hands in action

But your tongue too fast may run

And the lecture you deliver

May be very wise and true

But I'd rather get my lessons

By observing what you do

For I might misunderstand you

And the high advice you give

But there's no misunderstanding

How you act and how you live.

How do you act around your children? How do you carry yourself? How do you speak to them? What words do you use and in what tone do you speak them? Children do not perceive the world the same way adults do. In order for children to learn values from their parents, the parent must demonstrate the behavior first. You must be what you want your child to become.

Chapter Five

America Has
A Culture Problem:
Hip Hop

5
America Has
A Culture Problem:
Hip Hop

The purpose of this chapter is to show the impact hip-hop culture has had on innocent children, turning many of them into deviant rebels and the negative impact it has had on society as a whole.

Worldview

If you go to Chinatown in San Francisco, you will quickly learn that everything about the Chinese, regardless if they're US citizens or not, show that their language, dress, food, and their customs are from another place.

Walk around Chinatown, and you will suddenly realize that you cannot find a hotdog stand anywhere and nobody is speaking English. Most of what happens in America is foreign to their way of doing things.

It's not necessary to travel halfway around the world to learn what life is like in China. The Chinese in Chinatown have a culture and a worldview that they regard as sacred and are not willing to compromise that belief system even while living in America.

What Is A Worldview?

Worldview is as necessary for thinking as air is for breathing. You can't think in a vacuum, just like you can't breathe without air. Most of the time, you take the atmosphere around you for granted. You look through it, rather than at it, even though you know it's there. Much of the same goes for your worldview. Normally you look through it, rather than at it.

Usually it sits in the background of your thoughts, or as in most cases, you are never conscious of it at all. It is always present, always active, and it always influences your behavior. Therefore, a worldview is an overall view of the world as a person sees it through his frame of reference.

The hip hop culture has its own worldview. It's not a physical entity of the physical world. Instead, it's a philosophical view of thoughts and feelings about the spiritual, self, others, and the world around it. The world around you is quite different than the world around me. Some things are the same, but many things are different.

Two people can see the same police officer and walk away with a totally different meaning of what they just saw. One sees an enemy and the other sees a friend. Two people can see a Muslim and interpret what they see differently. We see with our eyes, but we interpret what we see through our worldview, our frame of reference.

A person may be educated or uneducated, Democrat or Republican, rich or poor, nonbeliever or God-fearing, but they all live and act in different ways based on how they see the world. The conflict in Washington, D.C. between Democrats and Republicans over gun legislation is the result of each party having conflicting worldviews.

Your worldview shapes and informs your experiences in the world. It affects not only what you see but how you see it. It's an inner perception of things. The fact that a liberal is a liberal and a conservative is a conservative is an indication that they both differ in how they see the same world and how they interpret what they see.

Kashawn Davis, a follower of hip-hop culture, does not see life, or the world, the same way a Wall Street banker does. Each has a general belief that forms a big picture or a grand perspective on life. The behavior stemming from their different views about life will produce different outcomes. The content of their conversation is different. Their lifestyle is different. The family values are different. The choice of music and dress is different. Each group believes based on their worldview, the way they see life is the right way life should be seen.

A worldview can be either positive or negative. It can either build a positive community or tear one down. A wholesome worldview based upon healthy thought patterns, moral values, a constructive belief system, and upright behavior usually produces a positive and productive lifestyle for those under its influence.

A contaminated worldview based on immoral values, violent and evil thought patterns, a profane regard for what's sacred, a distorted and misleading belief system may produce a dysfunctional and destructive lifestyle for those under its influence.

The adverse, rebel culture of hip-hop has in many ways adversely influenced innocent children, infusing them with misinformation and misguidance through music and lifestyle. This counter culture constantly makes right look wrong and wrong look right, and our children believe it. The direct and indirect messages of this culture communicates that good is evil and evil is good, and our children believe it. These innocent ones, our children, are being programmed and conditioned, informed and misinformed, by a culture that does not seem to have a child's best interest at heart. A culture that is driven by greed and fame and makes excuses to justify the destruction of lives all around them.

Pause for a moment and reflect on one good thing that has come out of this culture to make our sons and daughters fit members of society. I haven't been able to find one. Instead, it has made disrespectful children more disrespectful, vulgar kids more vulgar, angry kids defiant, and violent kids more violent.

The children in public schools across America reflect these behaviors toward parents, teachers, and each other, and no one wants to admit why. We would rather stick our heads in the sand and side step the issue because we fear those who control this industry or the repercussions that might come as a result. Where is the love for our children and their future? The culture and its music may have made some temporary millionaires, but at what cost and at whose expense? Our children are the victims.

It would appear to me that any influence we have over our undeveloped babies would be to protect them rather than destroy them, that's if our motives were coming from a pure place. If this destructive outcome is the only contribution that the hip-hop culture can offer innocent children, then this culture leaves nothing for the oppressors to do, because this culture is doing everything for them. This rebel culture forms a destructive set of beliefs and values by which our children live their lives and the end is usually not a pretty one.

Some would say that it's not hip-hop but gangster rap that is the problem, but I believe that the disrespect for authority, violence, defiance and the profane towards the sacred is paraded throughout the hip hop culture. The attitude towards society, the world, and even their own people has much to be desired.

I would hasten to say that not all children exposed to the hip-hop culture and its music are affected negatively and become murderers as a result. But many of those kids who are not driven to the extreme still go through life as damaged goods, bound by their rebel thought patterns and conditioning that prohibits them from having healthy relationships with family and friends.

You can't make wise choices when you are programmed and conditioned with wrong and deceptive information. Proverbs 14:12 says: *"There is a way that seems right unto a man, but the end thereof are the ways of death."*

The Damage it Has Inflicted

Since the inception of hip-hop and gangster rap, the United States has seen more than 500,000 homicides, according to the United States Department of Justice. How many teenage murderers were influenced by the music that has conditioned them to be viloent and kill? How many more children and Nipsy Hussle's will we lose within the next ten years by the influence of this same culture?

The excuse is given that rap music, as we know it today, provides a voice for the voiceless, and they want their stories to be told. But I say that words and music are transformative in nature. They create strongholds in our thought patterns and alter our pattern of behavior. If you hear the profane over and over again and see images that are violent and demoralizing over and over again, then you become what you expose yourself to.

Their is no excuse when we look at the consequences of the stories being told in the music and the impact it's having on young minds, which is resulting in blood flowing in our streets. The stories in the music, that must be told, forces our kids to be stuck in the middle of the plot and storyline and keeps them in a bondage they can't escape.

The music traps them and they become bound by strongholds with no counter messages, from that music, that programs or redirects them into a brighter tomorrow. No talk about what a redemptive lifestyle could be like once the story of the streets has been told. Let's stop ignoring the distribution of this misinformation and sow the seeds of pure values in the hearts of these young innocent ones before another life is taken.

It's not about telling the story as much as it is about the money that is being made, and many artists are taking advantage of it by the exploitation of our kids. If many rappers were given a choice, they would choose money and fame over the destiny of their own children. We can clean-up the music if for no other reason than for the sake of our children. It can be done. It must be done. Our future depends upon it.

Chapter Six

The Music Has Gone Too Far

6

The Music
Has Gone too Far

What started as a wholesome, creative, innovative, and brilliant genre of music, has now turned the corner and has taken our society into an immoral state of disrepair. The music and entertainment industry continues to have an enormous impact on the minds of children. In many ways it has become the new Bible, by serving youth, like that of religion. Kanye West is a strong proponent of this philosophy.

Young people who are searching for identity take on this industry's values and belief system, and they chase after a lifestyle that does not belong to them. Young people look at the behavior of celebrity rappers as their code of conduct. They seek to match what they see as a perfect lifestyle. Fame and fortune become the standard by which they gauge success. Their whole life is wrapped around this illusion.

The Profane and its Impact on Society

Profanity has always been around in American culture but used to be frowned upon in most circles. Since when did it become acceptable for children and adults to be profane? You see parents cursing their children, and children cursing adults. How did blatant profanity seep into Hollywood movies, prime-time television, music, and music videos? Since the inception of rap music, profanity in most cases has become accepted as part of mainstream America. This is another example of how evil has become the new norm.

Profanity, as defined by Merriam-Webster, is an offensive word or language. It is also called bad language, foul language, swearing, or cussing. It is generally considered to be impolite, rude, or offensive. It can show debasement of someone or something or show intense emotion.

Profanity in the olden days was considered to be sacrilegious. It showed disrespect for the sacred. It was an affront against God. It showed that the user does not respect God or holy things. Today, because of the profane, our society to a large degree has become anti-God and carries a sacrilegious disposition towards the sacred, and many in our society are behaving as such. There is a slack in the mention of the word "GOD" and now, the phrase, "THE UNIVERSE" has moved God over and is now sitting in His chair. There should be no question about our moral decline and why there's so much violence and corruption in America.

When hip-hop introduced the explosive and flamboyant use of profanity into American culture, without any restrictions or filters, it was at first received with opposition and disdain by the vast majority. But when this vulgar contaminated language was repeated over and over again, every day, for weeks, months, and even years, especially in the form of music and video images, we have become desensitized.

The culture makes good look evil and evil is played up as something good. There is a demonic overcast that has spilled over into the whole of American culture and has the country in moral decline. It seems like there is nothing we want to do about it. We are blindsided and in a dark place by an evil outlaw spirit that engulfs us without any awareness of our condition nor the depth of our bondage. We have eyes that cannot see and ears that cannot hear.

America has let her guards down and has adjusted to the programming and conditioning of our minds without any awareness that it has happened. We would probably never admit it, but we have also become damaged goods by settling into a comfort zone. We are not much bothered anymore by the behavior or language we hear around us. It has become the new norm. The vulgar explosion has blown the eye sockets out of our heads and we walk in spiritual darkness. No longer are we able to tell the right from the wrong or willing to resist or condemn it.

I am reminded of the story about the frog who was placed in a pot of hot water. The frog immediately hopped out upon contact because of the heat. However, when another frog was placed in a cold pot of water, it did not leap out immediately. Instead the water was gradually heated, ever so slightly, over extended periods of time. With each elevation of temperature, the frog's body adjusted and became accustomed to the rising degrees of heat, leaving the frog completely unaware of the life-threatening danger waiting for it up ahead. The frog was boiled alive.

Gradual Captivity

The programming and conditioning process is so gradual and unnoticeable that before you know it, you are embracing elements of this destructive culture. The conduct that was once seen as deplorable is no longer unpopular. Blindness has set in, darkness has engulfed us, and now we become defenders of the darkness we once despised.

Even worse is when there is no realization of that blindness or darkness that has overtaken us. We can't see it or recognize our condition because of it. We have been programmed by an outlaw spirit designed to destroy the whole of us. This is deception at its highest level being enacted in an unseen world by unseen influences. Your innocent children grow-up with this all around them.

How can we celebrate rap stars on music award shows, with teardrops tattooed under their eyes, knowing what that tear drop stands for? It indicates that some mother's son or some father's daughter was murdered at their hands and we celebrate and elevate them to celebrity status. We then make excuses for our actions on their behalf.

How can something so dark be given so much acceptance? We hate the vulgar and adverse characteristics we condemn in Donald Trump but are numb when we see the same moral collapse and vulgar behavior in the hip-hop generation. We say we care about our children, but do we really? This rebel culture has caused us to lower our guards and our standards and we don't even know why. Like the frog in the pot, destruction has slipped up on us unnoticed. If you hear a lie, often enough, you may soon believe that lie to be true.

Donald Trump introduced the term "fake news," which was received by the masses with much skepticism. However, with constant usage of the term, Americans have now become skeptical of most news outlets. We don't know what or who to believe anymore. Trump has sought to change the perception of the world through repetition, and he's succeeding in his mission.

Innocent children, who are defenseless, are being led to believe that being a gangster, or displaying disrespect is the way things should be done.

When rap music is constantly being played in the home of a newborn child, the culture in that home becomes contaminated; and because the parents can only see with their physical eye, they are oblivious to the damage being done.

The negative atmosphere surrounding a child shapes their inner spirit into a distorted human being, who grows up angry with an unnatural appetite towards violence.

The culture of hip-hop is a distortion of reality. It is a deceptive and misleading lifestyle that has no productive ending. Many of the artists who become wealthy from it don't end up in a positive place, when all is said and done. What are the goals of this culture? Can they be defined? What are the values of this culture, the priorities of this culture? What is the upside that this culture is creating for our children and for the next generation?

I believe, in part, that the Hip-Hop subculture has played a significant role in the moral decline of American culture. The decline has already been cast on America even before Trump became President. When he became President, he walked into an already contaminated society, which made it easy for him to thrive. This adverse, rebel culture has promoted a lifestyle that has not been healthy for our children. It has been misleading and deceptive, to say the least.

Chapter Seven

Believing
and Living a Lie

7

Believing
and Living a Lie

When the Blind Lead the Blind

Suppose you were encouraged by your peers to jump off the Empire State Building and by doing so, experience a sensation you had never felt before. Your peers tell you about the thrill of flying on thin air, and the exhilaration is something that has no equal.

Your curiosity gets the best of you as they tell you of others who have done it before. Even though no one has returned to share the outcome of such a venture, they are just excited by the thought of it. The mystery of the unknown, the risk, and the rush that comes with it pushes you to the edge.

At the height of the temptation and the pull of peer pressure egging you on, you decide to take the leap. Not 100% sure of what you were getting into, you feel that if something bad happened to the others who jumped, nothing bad would happen to you. It just won't. After all, the people who are telling you to jump are trusted friends. They've never let you down before. They have always had your back. Why would it be any different now. So, you tiptoe over to the edge of the roof and with a deep breath and arms raised high above your head, you jump.

On your way down you discover everything they said you would experience was true, but it was far greater. Mid-way into the fall, however, you have an epiphany, like a lightning bolt from heaven, and it jars your reality. What in the world am I doing? Did I make the wrong decision? What if there is danger or even death that awaits me at the bottom of this jump? Maybe I shouldn't have listened to them? What if I've been deceived by friends who themselves have been deceived, not knowing the full truth? What if I never see my family again?

At that very moment, you have a change of mind. A paradigm shift has overtaken you. You want to turn back the clock, put the car in reverse, and go back to the top of the building. You pray to God, something you had never done before, begging Him to get you out of the mess you've gotten yourself into.

You continue your fall at high speed. You want to make a U-Turn back up the building to safety, but to your dismay, it's too late. You can't undo what's been done. The decision is final. You have reached the point of no return.

To ill-informed parents and misguided youth, there are some choices we make in life where there are no second chances.

The consequences are fixed and this is one of those cases. You can't undo what you've done. You can't make it right.

As ridiculous as this may sound it is the plight of many young people who have chosen the wrong friends or made bad choices. Choices that will lead to a destructive end. They have taken the leap over the edge heading to certain doom, and for some, there is no turning back. The point of no return has been reached. There is something that drives them every day in the wrong direction and to an unavoidable death. For some reason, they can't stop themselves from doing the wrong things. Strongholds bind them.

The problem with deception is that you do not know you are being deceived. It is the road you have chosen without knowing you have chosen it, nor what the end will be. Many will go to their graves never figuring it out.

The Pig in the Pen

I'm reminded of the man who felt sorry for the pig in the pigpen. He goes over to the filthy, muddy pig, and takes him out of the pen to a nice upscale room, in a plush hotel on the other side of town. When they reach the door of the hotel room two beautiful maids usher the pig into the bathroom, where a bubble bath awaits him. The two maids wash the pig down from head to toe until he is sparkling clean, and covered with rose pedals.

After the soothing bath, they escort the pig outside to a table, where he is placed to be pampered with a massage all over his body, administered with the finest of oils. After being dried off, the pig is diced with perfume, and a ribbon is placed around his neck.

The pig is then taken outside. All his pockets and luggage are stuffed with money by those who care. After experiencing a total transformation, he now has a chance to rise high above what life was like in the pigpen. He is set free to embark upon a life with enough financial resources to hold him down and knowing there is much more where that came from.

Many days pass, and the team responsible for the pig's transformation are anxious to see how he is doing in this new life he has been awarded. What opportunities has he been able to acquire now that he has changed? The team searches the streets, the parks, and the alleys, but the pig is not there. They search the houses and the hospitals in the area, but the pig is nowhere to be found. Nobody has seen or heard from him. Days pass into weeks, and weeks into months to no avail. Fear grips the hearts of the searchers. Where could he be? Could he be hurt? Could a family have killed and eaten him?

The moment when the team was exhausted and ready to give up, they decided to go back to his old neighborhood. They felt the pig would never return to that place after all the good he had been exposed to, but the team went there anyway. To their surprise, they found the pig right back in the pigpen where he had first been found. He was muddy, filthy, dirty from head to toe, and broke.

But why would he return to the pigpen after being exposed to the better side of life? Why would he give that all up? The answer: he is a pig. He does what pigs do because it's his nature to do so. Jeremiah 13:23 says: *"Can the Ethiopian change his skin, or the leopard his spots? How can you do good when you are accustomed to doing evil."*

Young people who are programmed to be profane, disrespectful, and violent are bound to these behaviors. It's embedded. They can't help themselves from doing what they do. It is a part of who they have become. You can lock them up in prison for ten years, set them free and they will go right back to the pigpen. Like the pig, it's their nature.

Transformation Comes Through the Renewing of The Mind

Deviant youth can't stop being who they are unless they hit a brick wall and an epiphany takes place in their heads. A light bulb comes on and they experience a paradigm shift in their thinking. You can't see when you are blind. You don't enjoy light when you are engulfed in darkness. Someone must shine a bright light in the darkness allowing you to find your way into a new lifestyle. John 8:22 *"Then you will know the truth, and the truth will set you free."*

Transformation can only take place when the mind is renewed. The mind can only be renewed when it is exposed to the light of truth. The only way to change the violent behavior of high-risk youth across America is not more cops, not more programs, and not even incarceration, but to change how they think and what they believe. Any other attempts will fall short of complete transformation.

Chapter Eight

The Profile of a Teenage Killer

8
The Profile of a Teenage Killer

D r. Helen Smith, forensic psychologist, shares the experience in her book *The Sacred Heart* about Xavier, a twelve-year-old who was locked up in a Tennessee juvenile detention center for murder. He had killed a man in cold blood by shooting him several times through the head at close range. One impulsive act, to prove to his friends that he was now a man, had ruined his life forever.

His father left his family when he was three and his mother took out her anger towards him by being very abusive. She remarried a man, who was also abusive to her, frequently beating her.

One day, when Xavier's stepfather was physically abusing his mother, Xavier jumped into the fight with a knife in hand, attempting to help his mother, only to have her turn on him. She took sides with his stepfather and put Xavier out of the house and into the streets. The streets became his home. He had little or no adult supervision. He started to drink and do drugs, which had an impact on his school attendance and behavior, forcing him to have to change schools thirteen different times.

Xavier witnessed three murders in his neighborhood, and the act of murder intrigued him. Finally, his chance came. When he was high on drugs, he killed a man. He thought it was a game and thought the police would let him go like they always did, but this time they didn't.

Too Young to Know

To analyze his level of disturbance, Dr. Smith asked Xavier to make three drawings. He was asked to draw a picture of a boy, a girl, and a picture of himself. He did as he was told, and this was the result. The male had hands, the female had no hands; which symbolized that he felt men had more power over women, which was no surprise, given the physical abuse he witnessed his mother endure at the hands of his stepfather.

In the picture of himself, he had facial features, eyes, mouth, ears, and hair. The boy and girl, on the other hand, had no facial features whatsoever. When Xavier was asked, he was unable to tell anything about them. He couldn't tell how old they were, what they enjoyed doing, or what were they like.

Xavier's drawings indicated that the boy and girl were nameless, faceless beings, who were nothing more than objects. This was an indication that he didn't see people as possessing qualities that make them special and unique.

People had no worth and no value. Kids who kill devalue and dehumanize people in general. To them, you are a NO PERSON. You don't count. They put distance between themselves and a person's humanity.

The average person cannot just go around killing people for the fun of it. We were not created with the propensity to take another human being's life. Something had to happen in Xavier's head to flip the switch. Let me explain what happens with many teenage killers in massive school shootings across America.

Military Conditioning

Colonel Dave Grossman, author of *Stop Teaching Our Kids to Kill,* states that in World War II only 15 percent of soldiers in combat were willing to fire their rifles at the enemy. That meant that eighty five percent of the soldiers found it very difficult to point their rifles and kill the enemy. This concerned military administrators, so they discovered ways to program and condition soldiers to help them overcome an innate resistance to killing another human being.

The first thing the military administrators did was to put certain systems in place to train soldiers to dehumanize the person at whom they were shooting. Infantry training during World War II used bull's eye targets to train soldiers, but that had to change.

They went from bull's eye targets to being trained to fire at realistic, man-shaped silhouettes, strategically placed into their field of view. Later, it was referred to as virtual reality. The soldier only has a split second to engage the target. The conditioning process was to shoot the target, it drops and pops up, shoot again, it drops and pops up; this action occurs repeatedly. It is known as stimulus-response.

Soldier practice this procedure thousands and thousands of times, until the act becomes a subconscious act. You now pull the trigger instinctively without any conscious thought.

At the time of the Viet Nam War, ninety five percent of the soldiers were now capable of killing. What made the difference?

The four steps the military used to turn soldiers into killers:

1. Programming and conditioning the soldier, through the act of repetition.

2. Desensitize the soldier, and then numb the brain.

3. Dehumanize the person being killed.

4. Devalue the life of the person.

I heard an eight-year-old boy, while I was teaching school one day, say to me emphatically, more than once, that he couldn't wait until he became an adult. He said it with such passion and with a sparkle in his eyes. I finally asked why was becoming an adult so important to him. He told me that he just wanted to know what it would feel like to kill somebody.

This boy was a video game enthusiast and experienced the splattering of blood and the killing of people everyday. He became conditioned. The virtual reality images he was shooting everyday dehumanized human life and caused him not to value life in the real world. He was ready at that age to kill. It is just a matter of time.

Many kids who enter schools with weapons to kill have had a great deal of practice at home. Their computers became their training ground that prepared them for this execution. These kids are experiencing the same psychological and emotional conditioning that soldiers experience in military training.

Friendly Fire

During the Gulf War, only 148 soldiers lost their lives, but 24 of those deaths were caused by friendly fire. The soldiers were trained so well to shoot at moving targets that when their own men would pop up in view, they would shoot them instinctively without any conscious thought. The act of killing was embedded in the soldier's subconscious mind. They were on auto pilot. They were programmed and conditioned to pull the trigger first and think later.

Military men in the USA, who join the police force after they are released from the military, tend to still have a thirst to kill. They shoot instinctively, without conscious thought when feeling threatened even when the threat is only a perception, and not a threat at all. Many of these soldiers should never be allowed to join the police department. They have mental challenges and should be treated before given a weapon in civilian life. They are a menace to society.

All kids who play video games won't turn into killers, but it's the few who can't safely manage the subliminal conditioning, and it takes them over the edge. Parents must be sensitive to the signs. There are always signs but most people don't pay attention to the atmospheric conditions surrounding their child's behavior, attitude and disposition. Pay attention!

I mentioned in the introduction about Kashawn Davis, on death row for the murders of two neighborhood acquaintances. Kashawn, like all kids, was born innocent, pure, and undefiled, with a blank brain, hard drive, and no data entry. He came into this world with a need to be loved, a need to belong, to understand and be understood.

His life ended the way it did because of how it began. Dysfunctional parents cannot raise a functional child. Kashawn's parents did not know how to raise a relationally healthy child. It doesn't mean that his parents were bad people; they just didn't know. They were not equipped with the knowledge to develop a healthy culture in the home, which was in their power to do.

Parents can't give what they don't have. If both parents are entrenched in a broken and fractured relationship with each other then they bring and raise their child in that brokenness. Kashawn Davis became a product of his environment. Many kids who are born innocent are adversely programmed by the culture that they were exposed to in the home as well as the culture that influenced them outside of the home. Change the culture save the child.

It's amazing how two kids can be born and reared in the same dysfunctional environment; one goes to college, the other goes to jail. One is wired one way; the other's wiring is quite different. The child who goes to college does not always escape his dysfunctional childhood conditioning completely. It may appear on the outside that he does, but he doesn't. Even though he gets those educational degrees and ends up with a good job, he will soon discover dysfunction in his relationship with others, and inadequacies in his relationship with his wife and children. Dysfunction in our childhood will show up in adulthood, one way or another, some more severe than others.

Kashawn's parents, unfortunately, brought him into an environment of dysfunction, and emotional neglect. They spent very little quality time with him. His parents were unaware of that neglect and the consequences it would have on their innocent child's future

When a child develops anger, disrespect, or even violent tendencies during those formative years, and he meets friends in his neighborhood with those same tendencies, together they usually take these deviant behaviors to the next level. To summarize my position is this book, Kashawn was born innocent and undefiled, but a product of his environment. The atmosphere, climate, and culture that he inherited laid the foundation for what he was to become.

Chapter Nine

The Only Place
Where Truth is Found

9
The Only Place
Where Truth is Found

Two Kinds of Knowledge

It is important that children are raised in an environment that has been seasoned with the positive elements necessary to make the atmosphere, climate and culture in the home conducive for the raising of a healthy and balanced child. Each family should have a spiritual standard to live by. A standard that governs both parents and children's behavior in the home and outside of the home.

There are two kinds of knowledge that confronts families in the world today. There is sense knowledge, which programs the head, and spiritual knowledge, which programs the heart. What are you pouring into your child in the form of verbal and non-verbal information? When parents want to decide the kind of information they want to expose their children to, they need to make sure that it comes from a pure source. It should be principled and morally driven.

You can't believe every book that you read, follow every leader that you hear, digest every movie that you see, nor take the advice from every friend that you have. What kind of information you allow in your home should be filtered, through a standard you have adopted for your home. Take it for what it's worth, I believe in the God of the Bible the **SOURCE** of all **TRUTH.** Anything else is substandard, in my opinion.

The Author of a Thing Defines That Thing

In a world where there are so many different opinions about how life should be lived, can truth really be known? It is the goal of the outlaw spirit to infuse the world with conflicting religious and philosophical ideas, so that God's true way gets buried in the rubbish and becomes more difficult to discern.

Whatever seems right to a person is what he is encouraged to do. It's "YOUR TRUTH", that everyone is encouraged to follow. Well, Donald Trump is living "HIS TRUTH" and look what happens. What are the consequences to others when a person with a contaminated heart has the liberty to "LIVE THEIR TRUTH?"

Because we all have our different concepts of truth, why should anyone be concerned about the man whose "TRUTH" leads him to drive his car on the wrong side of the interstate, against oncoming traffic, destroying the lives of innocent people, simply because he's decided to "LIVE HIS TRUTH"? That's what he wants to do, and so he does it. Is he to be punished for "LIVING HIS TRUTH"?

It is nonsensical to believe that we can be safe in a world filled with broken people and expect all to do the right things without a set of rules or boundaries to regulate how we should act and behave. Boundaries must be set not for some but for all when it comes to the safety of humankind. In many dysfunctional homes, boundaries and rules are not a priority.

Boundaries or rules can be defined as a regulated way of doing a thing. In order to be safe, we must know the right way of doing things in a world filled with people carrying different opinions. Driving a car in America is regulated by laws meant to keep us all safe. Lines in the middle of the road protect us from oncoming traffic moving in the opposite direction. Signs that tell us to yield, slow down, or stop are established for our protection.

What would things be like if there were no rules? There would be chaos, to say the least, and death on every corner. So, the people who believe they can do as they please, ignoring regulated boundaries, have put us all at risk. We are no longer safe in our homes, walking down the street, or stopping our car at a red light.

Who makes the rules? Who enforces the rules? Who decides if the rules are wrong or right? A person in power does. A person who knows the significance of forming such rules and is in a position of authority to enforce them. No one will follow the rules given by a person who does not have the power to enforce them.

No Need to be Misguided by Misinformation

I believe we can all know the moral universal standards by which we should live our lives. There's only one way to fly a plane, and that's the truth of the matter. Any misinformation in flying instructions could be deadly.

In order to find truth, we must go back to the beginning of all things, where all things originated. Where else can truth be found? Only the author of a thing can define that thing. The author in this context can be defined as the Originator or the Creator.

It was the Wright Brothers who gave definition and operational instructions for the airplane, and nobody debated them. Garrett A. Morgan who invented the traffic light, gave definition and operational instructions for it. Many people may have had their opinions, but it was not up for debate. Only the author of a thing can define the thing in which he created.

What God creates, He owns, what God owns, He instructs. He instructed the rain and the sun, along with other things to grow food. It was written in their DNA. He instructed the cow to produce milk. He instructed the chicken to lay eggs. He instructed man to be fruitful, multiply and to replenish the earth.

God's Legal Right

God, the Author of "ALL THINGS," has a legal right to define, and give the operational blueprint, to all that He made. My wife, who is in the medical field, has taught doctors from all over the world how to do robotic surgery. She used a system established by its creators called Di Vinci Surgical System.

It came with instructions on how the robot should be assembled and operated, down to the minutest detail. No one else was better equipped to lay out the operations and maintenance like the creators. It was their baby. They came up with the idea, hired designers and engineers to produce a working product that services humanity well.

It is God who made the grass, sky, water and sun, He created the human body with multiple functions. Therefore, the purpose and operations of what man needs to do on earth, in order to survive and be happy, must come from God. He is the Author. He wrote the textbook. He can no longer be ignored or denied in the affairs of man. If ignored it will be at our own peril.

"Train-up a child in the way he should go, and when he is old, he will not depart from it."

Proverbs 22:6

The Author of All Misinformation

God created Adam to see only the good in His creation, to the point where nakedness had no shades of evil. How could nakedness be a non-issue in one moment and a major issue the next? In the beginning all things were made good and pure, and nakedness was no exception. Negativity was nowhere to be found in the universe. No hospitals, no cemeteries, no dead leaves falling from trees, no biting dogs, nor stinging bumblebees. The bad and negative had no place in God's perfect world.

That was until Satan came along and caused man to partake of the forbidden fruit. Adam went contrary to the Master's plan. That was his choice, and with every choice comes consequences, especially when you've been given warning. When we diverge from the God's plan, we can expect no difference. Satan presented to Eve truth mixed with error, a misrepresentation of God.

Truth that deviates from its pure form is not truth at all. It is deceptive, it is misleading, and our children are victims of a world that leads them down the wrong paths in life, and to an undeserved doom. It is Satan's goal to mislead. If your eyes are not wide opened, you will fall into a pit.

Like the frog who was boiled alive, it happened so gradual that the conditioning is undetected. Even the best of us have become victims of the toxic culture surrounding us.

Misinformation was the tool used in Eve's deception and that same tool is being passed on from generation to generation.

Adam and Eve's nakedness, once looked upon as pure and holy, now had a negative connotation and that nakedness had to be covered up. The appearance of nakedness hadn't changed, but the perception of it had. What was perceived as good, was now perceived as evil.

A Paradigm Shift

After the fall of man, Adam was now looking at God's pure and holy creation through the eyes of an insurrectionist. Satan's concept had become Adam's frame of reference. Satan is the father of rebellion, disobedience, lies, and the profane. His ideology is the opposite from that of the Creator. To Satan, good is bad and bad is good. Wrong is right and right is wrong. Lies are truth and truth are lies. Everything God made good, the devil has perverted.

Adam had now taken on Satan's worldview. This distortion has followed us down through the ages and has found its appearances in the philosophies and counter religions of the world. A scheme of Satan, to lead humankind down the pathways of destruction.

"There is a way that seems right unto a man, but the end thereof is the ways of death." Prov. 14:12

Jesus said, *"Ye shall know the truth, and the truth will set you free."* John 8:32. He further states, *"I am the WAY the*

TRUTH and the LIFE, no man comes to the Father but by me." John 14:6

Disobedience immediately changed the perception of how they saw things. It was all about perception. God wanted man to see things from a pure and undefiled frame of reference.

Is there a source of information in the world that, if heeded, will turn murderers and criminals into law-abiding citizens? Is there any solution that can rescue the Washington politicians out of the mess they have gotten us, as well as themselves, into? Is there any way this world can no longer be cursed by war? Can we find a source that can correct the racial issues that divide us? The answer to these questions is yes.

The Solution to Every Problem

Transformation comes when the mind is renewed. The mind is renewed when the light of truth invades the soul in darkness. To change the people in the world, and the

Kashawn Davis' of the world you must change how they think and in what they believe.

There is a Creative Wisdom that comes from God and from God alone, that can no longer be ignored or denied. God has a solution for every earthly dilemma, regardless, of how adverse that problem might appear to you. He had a remedy for darkness that we call light. He had a remedy for hunger that we call food. And He has a remedy for gang violence that I call knowledge, a knowledge that clears up misconceptions about how life should be lived. A TRUTH that will change how gang members think and in what they believe. Transformation is accomplished when the MIND IS RENEWED. The is no other solution.

A healthy and happy life is not established by money, or fame but through building healthy relationships with people, places, and things. Healthy relationships must encompass everything we do, and it will determine the quality of life we live on every level of human existence. You decide!

If the United States politicians want to improve the chaos that surrounds them, they must decide to improve their relationships with each other. Healthy relationships consist of love, respect, trust, and goodwill. These are relational attributes and spiritual attributes as well. If the government would focus on this one thing, what a wonderful world it would be.

Why do I bring up the significance of relationships as a cure for solving all the problems of humankind? Because God, the Author of all things, gave us this as a solution to all human problems. Here it is.

> *"You must love the Lord your God with all your heart, all your soul, and all your mind." This is the first and greatest commandment. A second is equally important: love your neighbor as you love yourself.*

Matt. 22:37-39

This is the call to all humankind. You were created for relationships by a relational God, who is "LOVE." You are shaped by your relationships. God summarizes man's total mandate on earth and raps it in the experience of healthy relationships. Produced by one word "LOVE."

Let's save our children, not with more programs or more prisons, but with "LOVE"

> *"Too much love, too much love*
>
> *Never in this world could there*
>
> *Be too much love.*

> …Wayne Hayes

Chapter Ten

The
Problem Can be Fixed

10
The
Problem Can be Fixed

I want to conclude with a word of hope. The greatest contribution that I want to make in this book is to answer the question of "WHY"? Why do deviant kids act the way they do? If your car doesn't start for whatever reason, you can't fix your car until you find out why it won't start.

The solution to a problem cannot be applied, until the cause has been uncovered. The issues we have faced in America, with kids who go bad, is we try to fix the problem without exploring and addressing why the problem exists. We hire more police officers, provide more after-school programs, more recreation, only to discover that the child's heart remains the same and his behavior never changes.

Some problems are surface problems and can be fixed in a few minutes, like a loose or corroded battery cable in your car, or a headlight that needs to be replaced. The ability to change the brakes on your car, or to replace a cracked radiator is possible for a novice mechanic, but who is not one who is equipped to handle the major issues. When the motor or transmission is in question, you need a specialist to handle the inside jobs. One who must go inside of the motor to determine if a loose part needs to be tightened, or if a broken part needs to be replaced, or if the motor needs a complete overhaul, and in the worst case even to be discarded.

A specialist who knows the inside workings of the issue will figure it out. That's what specialists do. The problem with innocent children who have gone wrong, is an inside problem that only a specialist can see and repair.

If the culture surrounding the innocent child caused his negative behavior, then we must plan to fix it at the place where the problem began. Culture determines the child's behavior. To neglect this is to fail on all levels. Remember, culture can be created or fixed. The tools to do so are at your disposal.

In my next book entitled, *How to Raise a Positive Child in a Negative Environment*, I will lead you step by step into a PARADIGM SHIFT, on how to reverse the negativity in your child's behavior and home environment to make the bad good and the good better. It will lead you out of the dark pit, helping you to see light at the end of the tunnel. The problem that your child is having, is relational in nature. There is a fracture in one or more of his relationships. Fix the fracture heal the child. Help is on the way. STAY TUNED!! There is more to come!!

What Turns Innocent Kids Into Ruthless Killers?

About the Author

Princeton H. Holt was born in Brooklyn, New York and attended elementary and high school in that city. He attended Oakwood University, in Huntsville, Alabama, and Andrews University Theological Seminary in preparation for pastoral ministry.

He started pastoring in South Atlantic Conference of SDA and immediately emerged as one of the leading soul winning pastors in that conference. He pastored sixteen churches over 40 years throughout the United States, planting three new churches in Georgia, North Carolina, and Tennessee.

He served as Youth Director for South Central Conference of SDA, where he trained and prepared, youth leaders in churches throughout the states of Kentucky, Tennessee, Alabama, Mississippi, and Northwest Florida, on how to successfully serve the youth in local churches and how to impact the lives of youth in their community.

While serving as Youth Director, he acquired a mobile theater and conducted outdoor theater productions, in public housing developments throughout the five states impacting thousands of youth and their families.

He Founded and Pastored, Dawn Christian Fellowship Community Church. He owned and operated a child development center, a housing development corporation, a global radio station, a theater company, and now serves as Founder, and CEO, of Agents of Change International, a movement designed to impact adverse cultures, wherever they are found.

He is married to the former Constance McKoy, they live in the northeastern part of the U.S.A., and they have three grown children.

Stay in Touch!

Stay in touch with Princeton H. Holt.
Listen to his broadcasts on radio and podcast.
princehholt@yahoo.com

For speaking engagements
http://www.princetonspeaker.com

For book purchases
princetonhauthor.com